Diablos:

Murder or

Suicide?

Michael Cocchiaro

Dedication

This book is dedicated to my father, Robert Michael Cocchiaro. May he continue to guide me as though he had never died.

Acknowledgment

With this book, I would like to thank my father, who has given his life in such a way.

CONTENTS

About the Author

I have never been able to get back to the day my father left; he was never able to return. I am just a son, a father, and with this book, I am also an author.

Page Blank Intentionally

Preface

Ever since my father's death, there hasn't been a single night when I could sleep in peace. Although I was not present there to witness the death scene, the thought of seeing him dead brings shivers down my spine. He was a great man and, more than that, the man of my life, my Big Poppa. What do a youthful wants from his life? A happy family and a successful high school and career? I knew my father might not be able to offer me that without hard work, education, dedication, and motivation, but I could look up to him for all the strength that I could ever need to make our lives well.

I had seen him struggle to do every bit of a thing he could to make up for all the wrongs he had done. His life was tough, and his challenges were more than I could even imagine. It is not easy to leave the streets where you have spent all your life and start a brand new one, but he did it only for the sake of his family. He was friends with the gang leader for years, even before he knew my mother. His life was at all times on the verge of breaking out because every time he would return from detention, we thought it would be a fresh start now, and at times it was so.

Furthermore, we moved to innumerable places to end his connections with the leading drug trafficking gang in Meriden, CT, the Diablos. But he was inextricably interwoven to everything the gang had to offer. Be it the trafficking of stolen cars and narcotics or the consumption and dealings of cocaine and heroin - my father was into everything. He was in and out of the rehabilitation as he wanted to give up his old self, which was compelled to addiction and secure his family's future. He went through breakdowns and had major relapses too. No matter how tough of a person he was, what I know is that he did not deserve to have an end like this. The way the police department pulled back their hands from the murder case of my father made me realize how they had been using my father all along. For years, the Southington police were in anticipation of raiding and charging the Diablos, and when they found my father, they got bait. The police were well aware of my father's vulnerabilities, and they knew where exactly to hit, and they did it very well.

The day my father was caught with a *38 special* revolver, he signed up for snitching on the Diablos, the gang he had known and hung out with for many years. Thanks to Cadillac Jack, who was otherwise known as Jackie or Jack Baltas in my house.

My father, the man who used to threaten people and fill their minds to brim with fear, was now helpless and troubled for the sake of his and his family's life. When he had worked enough on taping the trafficking deals by infiltrating the clubhouse, he sensed how big of a mistake he had made by cheating on his friend. Additionally, he knew if Jackie came back, he would rip his head off, so he decided to reveal to him the plans of the police and gain security for himself. But he ended up in disappointment as Jackie clearly said there was nothing he could do for him.

To this day, I do not know for sure what made my father fly to Florida after that. But what I know for sure is that he was set up to be killed. He did not go to Florida out of his own idea, but he was led there. Even a layman could tell, knowing the details, that it was by no means suicide but a murder.

However, the police wanted to wind up the case and show no association with my father or give him his sheer share of working as an informant. So, there was no investigation for my father's case. Also, the medical reports were not shared with us. A lie after a lie was presented to us, *"He died due to drug overdose," "He died due to asphyxiation," "He was found in the tub," "He was found hanging in the closet."* What not was said except for the truth.

During these 26 years of my life, I have banged every single door I could, met numerous people, and shook hands with street guys, only to get some clue to that one person who could admit his inhumane act of murdering my father. I had given up on the idea that the police would sort this out. Neither can I expect anything from the detective who was the first witness to my father's body, for I suspect his involvement in drug trafficking for many reasons. Also, I see him on his Facebook profile flaunting his pontoon planes to the Dominican Republic, the possible origin of drug trafficking. By owing a two-person detective firm, God knows how he could make six figures; perhaps the money comes from somewhere else.

Not a single man dared to speak up for justice to my father. Their one mistake had ruined my teenage. It has destroyed me as a child and brought an end to a family that was in the midst of living anew. They can by no means get me back the time I had invested in knowing the truth behind, and they can by no means make up for the loss I had to bear in every aspect of my life, be it education, personality, love, support, family and so much more. Therefore, through this book, I want to voice for nothing but a proper closure to my father's case. I demand a formal investigation and want the police departments to lay off respectfully my father's connection with them as an informant. I yen the police department to credit him for all that he has done for the sake of the federal department and, consequently, lost his life.

May the soul of my father rest in peace, and if not world, I believe the Lord will do justice to him, and his wrongdoer will indeed be paid back.

Chapter 1
It Started Around the 80s

"Suppressed by drugs and sex for treatment at the age of fifteen, trying desperately to get answers for all that happened to my father. I hit the streets when sex and drugs no longer satisfied my hunger for truth."

I am Michael Cocchiaro, born in 1980, and this book is about the expedition I took to uncover the truth. When I was fifteen years old, I lived at 32 Darling St. Apartment D in Southington, CT. I was the only son of my father. I have two half-sisters, and it was years later when I came to know I have a third one too. In the eighties, I grew up with two of my half-sisters, but they had both moved out during the nineties. At that time, my oldest sister was busy having children, and my other sister moved in with her boyfriend. They were in and out of the home. Tiffany would visit more often because Stacey was so busy with her children.

I was in the ninth grade at Southington High School. This was a huge accomplishment because my family has tussled for many years. We had been struggling to eat (besides school lunch). My father was involved in the streets, from coke to whores to buying and selling drugs, from the biker gang to assault and battery. So, for me being able to eat and have an adequate and peaceful sleep became an accomplishment at that time. I had plenty of struggles already; I had lost my best friends Bobby and Juney in a house fire; they were our next-door neighbors on village lane in the nineteen-eighties. My dad tried to save them but could not. Also, my dad was involved in undercover wiretapping for police narcotics detectives back in the eighties, risking his life. It was pretty scary for me back then.

Finally, it seemed like life was going to be alright. But I was an underdog. I was devastated by the way my father disappeared. I dropped out of high school and moved in with a lady named Jennifer, who comforted me with sex, and I began doing drugs too. Though I was underage, I started to smoke weed for mere medication to cope with the sheer shock I was in, the loss of my father. It killed me. Between the drugs and sex, I also began writing rhymes, trying to calm my nerves. But I eventually went back to high school for my mother.

I used to be the skateboarder in my school. My friend circle had a mix of friends, from the most popular to the weird ones. Most of the girls in high school loved me because I was the lady's kind of man, and it helped me to fill up my social life. I loved girls, music, and skateboarding. I was mostly in high honor classes and a graduate valedictorian from Platt in Meriden, CT. I tend to understand people that understand me.

My dad! He grew up in Meriden, Connecticut, out of a group home called the Curtis home. I am not sure why he was separated from his parents. My mother always tried to keep these details from me. Also, she encouraged my father not to share them; perhaps some disturbing arguments revolved around that subject. However, I had met my grandfather several times, my uncle and grandmother a few times only. I remember a few vacations when I was a kid. Once, we went to Florida and even Disneyland. I assume my father's mother, my grandmother, and my father's brother also lived in Florida.

My dad spent time with me, teaching me karate that he had learned from his brother. He would train me in the basement with weapons of all sorts when I was only five or six. Mostly hand-to-hand combat techniques, but my father was the type to be versatile with all kinds of weaponry. Also, breathing techniques; my dad taught me to focus and to learn breathing techniques at a very young age. He was a remarkable man until he began to hang around with the bikers from a well-known motorcycle gang Diablos.

At times, my father was an animal. One day my father and his friend Abe from the Village Lane in South Meriden were at the kitchen table with a giant lunch bag. The paper bag was filled with a large compact brick of pure hard white cocaine. I do not think I was supposed to know what they were doing, but I got to know anyways.

DIABLOS: MURDER OR SUICIDE?

My father had street ties from the city where we lived and with his friends, some of whom he had known even before I was born. They were a mix of gang members from a full spectrum, including the Diablos Motorcycle Biker Gang and their leader, Jackie Baltas, and Puerto Rican Dominican gang leaders from the city. Because my dad knew Latin gangs and biker gangs very well, he served as a bridge between the two of them and the biker's gangs in drug trafficking. My father seemed to be hustling very heavily about the mid-eighties; the paper bags full of white powder (cocaine) mostly bricked with the Puerto Rican leaders getting to the next level every time. This all was happening in a village in south Meriden, better known as village lane.

Things indeed got heavy. He started coming home with new cars like a convertible Red Fiat 500 and a nice Buick

DIABLOS: MURDER OR SUICIDE?

Skylark, electronics that were not even out yet, such as two-way face time technologies way back in like 1986. I informed my sister about this, and she asked me to just go with it. Nobody really knew, but my father got caught in some serious gang activity and was working for the boss. My father was incarcerated on felonies and was constantly in and out of rehabilitation centers because of drug overdoses. He was so indulged in drugs by this time. My father then went through a very long recovery process, and thankfully, he said goodbye to his friends; the Diablos, the biker gangs, and the street's Latin gangs. By now, he had realized all the wrong and so badly wanted to be a family man. At this point, he had a ponytail and arm full of tattoos but nothing that a collared shirt could not hide. Some of his tattoos could tell stories like the grim reaper with a head on a sickle or cemetery on his back with his own gravesite and tattoos of spider webs on his elbow that he got in jail.

Around the summer of 1995, my father worked for a steel company Ulbrich Steel in Wallingford, Connecticut; he probably worked with heavy metals stacking, shipping, and receiving orders. He was trying to do the right thing after several imprisonments throughout those times from the eighties. Unfortunately, he was injured and put out of work, given a nerve replacement and pain medication, but my mother was always by his side. She worked hard at Dunbar Armored Security, busy counting millions of dollars each day, to be exact, to support her family. My mother was the protector of her kids at this time and loved us so much. She was a super strong woman. My mother and father had a pretty good relationship early on; she loved him so much, and so did my father. Back in the eighties, my parents had us in church, Sunday school, and school all week long, though. We would eat meals at the kitchen table and clean our rooms till they were spotless.

For the most part, growing up, it did seem like they were good parents. There were times of sobriety too. But it just got so hard. There were many ups and downs, and my father and mother both became pretty abusive toward one another. I always had faith and prayed to Jesus a lot. They just wanted to work through their problems, and my mother wanted to keep my father out of jail and focus on how he did when they first started to raise me and begin their family. My mother would ask him if he needed help and even fought with him because of his bad decisions. She often accused him of having other relationships or being out with scumbags, Diablos, or old biker friends.

After the injury at the steel mill, my

father had a major relapse to some of his old Diablo biker friends that always had a healthy supply of drugs, guns, women, cars, whatever you needed basically.

Things were getting terrible now, and there was not that much charm of the summer left. I would be out with my best friend Ronnie at that time, trying to stay out of trouble. But even he was starting to sell weed. One day, my dad came with the cabby. This time he had a revolver - a .38 special along with a coffee-can of ammo. He was high on drugs and was not in his senses, and he wanted to fire them.

The Diablos were infamous for being involved in drug trafficking as well as firearms, sales of stolen goods, and just about every other major crime in a small city. I believe that the police had many good relationships with the diablos - I believe they still do. I also believe the police do not want a war in their streets. I do believe things got out of control, and my father had a big mouth because he didn't give a fuck; he didn't trust them to not set him up or kill him.

At this point, late at night, my father would try to explain to me the good and how he had just got the gun for protection and how he was going back to the VA hospital to detox and get on the right level of medication, so he would not need the street drugs. But the fighting continued between him and my mom. She was so bothered about who he was getting involved with again because she knew it was trouble. No matter what the Diablos did, they were big trouble for my father, and this proved to be so true.

My father had also found a whore he would go to. She lived not too far from the house where he could get high and do other things too, and my mother confirmed this when the police were investigating the biker's gangs. One day, my mother was yelling and screaming at him for having a relationship with a woman from up the street. I feel my mother was making a last-ditch effort trying to explain that love will conquer all because she loved him so much.

Chapter 2
Running with the Gangs

My father got involved with the gangs early on before he had married my mother. I was young and did not know everything, but it seems these Diablos are a part of my mom's side of the family or somehow related. My father was introduced to Diablo's leader Jackie Baltas at a rather young age, probably in his teenage. They both grew up in the city of Meriden, and as I was told, my father had known these people even before my mother or other family did. Since Diablos are very well known in my home city, my mother, sisters, and a few of my cousins know them. Now secretly enough, even today, my mother knows many of the diablos, and so does my sister.

Over time, my father had changed during his involvement with the Diablos. He was rather lowkey but dealing with the gang made him overt and sharp. Whether my father was stealing cars, selling drugs, or robbing people. But even though he wasn't the everyday biker gang member, my father was more of the loner type. My father basically stopped running with the Diablos biker gang in Meriden, Connecticut, when he was sentenced to prison for his part in a high jacking tractor-trailer truck with loads of merchandise. He was good with them, but he no longer needed to be at the grove street clubhouse or hang out, drink beer and get high by the fire type of guy anymore. Although his "in" with diablos was always supposed to be that he had an "out." He was left with no outs and was eventually found dead.

My father knew it was not safe to stick around with the Diablos, but he stayed loyal to people he felt were powerful. And Jackie was a mighty leader of a powerful gang. My dad had it good for knowing Jackie well, but he did not want to have the average pledge either. Therefore, he had a friendship with Jackie. Generally, the relationships of these biker gangs are business with any outsiders, but my father had known them for a very long time. My father did things for gang people he should never have. If the gang asked him to, he would steal, sell drugs, cars, and the money he did not care about because he had been doing this for Diablos. My father beat people up, threatened to kill people as well, and if he ever needed, these boys had his back.

My dad knew the city very well, and the diablos always have the connections for anything you may need. Gangs are designed to run in the streets, and the streets are filled with people. Our home city has like 70 thousand people and is surrounded by cities all similar in size. They had a widespread network. Easy on off-highway exits. Such places are for booming cartels and biker gangs running their bars, street stolen cars, and drugs. It is a wonder how these gangs are still presently established in my home city despite all the dirt they do.

At times my father was very aggravated. He was not the type of man who needed Jackie's name to hold onto for veneration when he was doing the things he was asked to do. The diablos loved my father's ruthless behavior to do anything, to say anything, and to slap his wife and kids' kind of thing. The gang fed off my father's liveliness, and in return, the gang obliged my dad.

DIABLOS: MURDER OR SUICIDE?

My father was not the mastermind or the leader of the gang. He was more like an entrepreneur who just wanted to be a gang member without actually being in the gang. He did not want to be an official member of the gang or the one that required his every second availability, as he did not want that lifestyle. Moreover, my father never wanted to associate the gang with his wife or children. On the other side, my father probably always thought he would use the gang as a scapegoat for his troubles if he were in hot water, but this would not necessarily be the case. Nevertheless, Jackie very smartly played on my dad and had him suffer at the hands of the police department for which my dad was working as an informant regarding the activities of Diablos.

Initially, my father knew the leader of the gang, and the diablos club was not his home like 99% of the rest of the gang members. My father was home and did not have to work for the gang, but he did keep in contact with them as he had known them most of his entire life as a kid growing up on the streets of Meriden, Connecticut. With the passage of time, when eventually his involvement with the gang grew more than an entrepreneur, he was beating his wife and kids, selling hard narcotics, shooting up heroin, and being a psychotic maniac in and out of lock-up and rehabilitation centers. Then, in the nineties, I think my father did a lot of things with the gang that I do not know about, especially in the eighties, as I was just too young. I know a few things about his involvement in stealing cars, dealing drugs, beating up people, and getting involved with street women.

Amidst all this, my mother and I suffered a lot. At times the fights were so severe between my parents that she struck my father to draw blood a few times, so did he. I remember when he would slap my mother or try to throw her out of a moving car. Either way, my mother had been through so much with him. But she was not giving up or going out like that even though the fights got serious during these times. Physical slapping, hitting shots to the face, throwing ashtrays, and all that type of stuff. My mother just begged him that she needed him to stop the street and gang crap and get a straight life to live. There were times when my dad was in rehabs getting the best care. We had visitation, but it was always so hard, so many tears, we just did not fully understand. My mother gathered herself in all these phases. She was a strong woman and had a huge heart.

Though I suppose privately, my mother was dabbling with social narcotic use in the eighties, but I also believe she left the drugs to raise her kids alone. Every day she had fought within herself, and my mother would pour her heart out in so many ways. If she was really angry, she could get violent herself. She cried and visited my father at the prison and went to rehabilitation centers to get help for my father. She has always worked hard to keep her vows to her husband. She has always loved and supported her home and children. There would be no food in the house, while my father would be in and out of jail and rehabs, my mother would work for long hours to be able to earn bread for her home. My mother fought so hard and warned him too. Everyone told him that we loved him so much, and the drugs were just too potent. Throughout this battle, there were a few times my father tried to make up for his relapse to my mother, like buying a camper and trying to have family time, but this would not last long either.

DIABLOS: MURDER OR SUICIDE?

The turning point came when in the nineties, my dad and other members were charged with embezzlement. They were caught stealing tractor-trailer loads of merchandise, fencing the product throughout the city, and when my father got out of prison for those charges, it was then when we were moving out of Meriden. I was moved all around Meriden, Connecticut as a child. We moved to Southington, Connecticut, then tried to get a clean and sober life, for my father needed that. He went to programs for sobriety. We always seemed to move when things got rough, and my father had incarcerations. Then it would happen again, and it kept going like this.

We had moved a lot too. It seemed to be what helped keep my father out of the gangs' streets and any trouble. Between two cities, we seemed to move every year or two. We moved into a new spot out of town in

DIABLOS: MURDER OR SUICIDE?

Southington, CT. Southington was the next town to Meriden, Connecticut, and more upscale from the streets to schools and bars. It was a classier town as opposed to the city. Jackie's business had no boundaries, and his gang was a coast-to-coast gang that originated in California. My father had traveled that way around the time I was born.

But maybe my father never stopped being friends with Jackie. He worked and possibly used or sold things acquired from the gang even when we moved to Southington.

Diablos must have been the go-to spot for my father if he needed anything fast and easy. The gang could provide pretty much anything the streets needed. So, reconnecting with Jackie was just a matter of taking the cab to the clubhouse on Grove Street in Meriden and seeing what the gang was up to.

The last time my father was at the

rehab, I don't believe my father ever had the full intentions of going back to the diablos like he needed to wear their colors red and black or sport their jackets or vests. He wanted to move on and start over, and that is why he started working at Ulbrich Steel for a better life for his family. He really wanted to leave the past behind and create a beautiful life for his family that seemed to be growing so rapidly.

Chapter 3
The Deal-breakers

We had moved to Southington, and my father had made it through his rehab programs. He was receiving outpatient care now through the Veteran's hospital. Alongside, my father began working at the Ulbrich Steel in Wallingford, Connecticut. I was just in middle school and would be meeting new friends again in the new town, and for a year or two, things seemed alright. At this point, maybe even too good. He wanted a fresh start, and it seemed like things were going to be okay now.

Apparently, he had left behind all his connections with the Diablos. My father has had several admissions in the rehabs already as he was indulged severely in narcotics. I did not want my dad to spend the rest of his life like this. Therefore, my mother and I have always been very patient with him. Every time my father was in or out of rehab, my mother supported him to the fullest. All she wanted him to do was get rid of hanging around with the biker's gang and not do things that could lead to severe consequences.

It was not only my mother or father but me too, who had been through a lot and suffered constantly. I was emotionally and mentally disturbed seeing my mother and father fight every other day to the extent that my father almost wanted to take my mother's life. He acted like a beast at times because he was so overdosed. I was too young at that time to be on an emotional roller coaster, but circumstances left me no choice. They left my mother no choice too. Along with working to win bread for life, my mother had to manage everything well. At times I would look at her and think how she could be so strong and not give up. But then I knew the answer because she loved my father and me even more than we could ever imagine. She wanted to make it till the end.

There were times when my father had relapses. All that my mother and I had worked on to get back to normal would go in vain. He would go back to his old life, visiting the clubhouse of Diablos and getting involved in all the evil that the gang did. Even to the worst, the gang might have been involved in people trafficking. Still, there were times when everything was seemingly alright, and we felt maybe we would be able to have normalcy. But fortune had to play its part. And we were struck once again by the miseries of my father's relapse. As my father was working at Ulbrich Steel, his work involved dealing with heavy metal stacking.

Unfortunately, he met an accident when a large, heavy metal sheet crushed a nerve in his elbow. He had no sensations and feelings and was set for surgery to replace the damaged nerve with a nerve from his knee and had to leave his job.

From here on, things never went back to normal. Not even apparently. Not even seemingly. While my father was struggling to recover from his nerve injury, the doctors put him back on high doses of pain medications, which happened around the mid-nineties. He would go back to the hospital for short periods for more medicine. He would frequently be visiting the Veteran's hospital around this time. He was in real pain. One can never imagine what we had been through. When eventually, he wanted to forget all his past and start anew for the sake of his wife and son's security, life bogged him down in the most miserable way ever.

27

DIABLOS: MURDER OR SUICIDE?

Around this time, he met a cabby named Andy who would give him free medical rides. After spending some time with him, he probably asked him where to score drugs and have alcohol while taking other Benzodiazepines and pharmaceutical drugs. Andy and my father would spend time together while my mother was at work, and we kids were busy for the summer with friends, playing basketball at the apartment complex on D Street in Southington. And to our greatest fear, he had his all-time major relapse. He would act like an animal, back to the streets, and even worse, he linked back with Jackie, the leader of the Diablos and he had got back into the drugs real good. Except for this time, it was not to be for the sake of profit but his use. There were times when I would come home to him, nodding out on the couch or locked in the bathroom. At this point, we believe he was pretty much shooting up heroin, getting very high, taking all his pain away.

My father started using them really badly. He was so high that sometimes he would pass out in the bathroom on the floor or vacillate between consciousness and unconsciousness while we tried to speak to him. We felt so helpless at times that we could do nothing but cry. After that, he began to act very weirdly and hang around with Andy in his yellow cab. He had now fully relapsed back to some of his old Diablo biker friends who always had a supply of drugs, guns, women, cars, whatever you needed basically. This cabby was well known, and I think he helped my father with rides to and from the gang's meeting spots while my mother was at work.

One day while my mother was at work, my father came home with a new car. This was very strange because we could not afford a new car. So, she asked him what dealership he got that car from? But my father would not tell her. However, deep inside, my mother knew it was happening because he had rekindled his old relationships with the Diablos. My parents began to fight with each other, and the abusive process started again. My father's awkward behavior did not stop at the purchase of his new car. Soon after, he showed me his new gun, a .38 special revolver that he had picked up. The firearm my father was carrying at this point was given to him by the cab driver, Andy. Ultimately that was the story I was told. Maybe he committed crimes with it, maybe it was for protection, or maybe it was planted on him given to him to arrest him later (this is the reason that I am most convinced of).

I do not know exactly why he even had that gun in the first place. He knew his life was so in danger at this point and that a gun was the last thing my father needed to have. This proved true because I could almost count the days from when he showed me the .38 special to the day he was found with it. He hid it from my mother, but he did show me how to load it up. He did not want her to be involved in this. My father was a felon and had been frequently in and out of jail. He was not allowed to have a firearm by law, or he would face prison. At this point, my father would make me sit with him late at night and explain to me how he had got his gun for his protection, and soon he would be going back to the Veteran hospital to get rid of all the drugs. He said he wanted to get on the right level on medication so that he did not have to take street drugs.

My mother became even more bothered about who he was getting involved with again because she knew it was trouble. No matter what, the Diablos for my father were trouble, and this proved to be true every time. Even though my father thought if he got in serious trouble, he would use the gang as the blame game and get rid of it. However, my mother was aware that this would not be the case.

One day as I came home to my mother and visited her upstairs in her room, she seemed confused, and I believe she was crying. She seemed very upset, and I was unsure what I had walked into. So, I asked her if everything was okay, and she said, *"Michael, it is your father; he is at it again, and I think he is with other women too. This has to stop."* She continued and said, *"he does not even love me anymore."* My mother was not okay with my father being out, God knows where. But she was way past worried. She knew too well what was going on, and this would enrage my father even more. He felt she did not trust him with his plans.

As we talked upstairs in the hallway, the front door swung open and smashed shut.

"Where are you?" my father yelled out.

"Upstairs," I said.

"There you are," he said.

"Where have you been?" my mother yelled at my father. *"How could you do this to your son? How could you hurt your wife so bad that you do not even love her anymore?"*

He was not even thinking straight because he was probably high. He did not appreciate this confrontation.

"Get the fuck out of my face and shut up. Quit talking like that in front of my son," my father yelled at my mother.

She wanted to have this as the precipitating event to make all things right, and she thought that getting hard on him and calling back with all love she has for him could actually have him give up all bad. So,

33

for a moment, I, too, felt the epiphany that this would be the breaking point. And it was. But who knew it was not the one in our favor? My father backhanded my mom's chest, knocking her to the floor. She screamed, *"Michael, he has got a gun,"* she tried to reach for his gun that was sticking out of his coat, then proceeded to the stairs. I followed him to the top of the stairs. He looked at me, dead in my eyes with his gun poking out of his long trench coat and his long ponytail with fire in his eyes; he cried out loud, *"You will never be man enough to face me."* I felt devastated and helpless at the same time. I saw the vulnerability in my dad's eyes. I wanted to cry at the top of my lungs.

They both went down the stairs out of the door, and he stormed up the road. I ran to my mother and then tried to follow my father up the street. My mother called the cops because she was so scared. She was frantic on the phone with the police. I followed him on my bike as fast as I could, but by the time I got past the apartments to the next street, the police had my father leaned over their car with the gun on the roof and his hands cuffed.

"Why?" I screamed so loud. He was going to jail, and it was all over. Tears began to roll down my eyes, and I cried for so many things. I was finished. I could not believe that my father got caught. My high school career was going to be over, and I had so many emotions rushing wildly into my nerves. When I got back home, I was so scared and upset. My mother tried to console me.

Shortly after my father's arrest, my mother was called to visit the Meriden police department. This is when we found out if my father was going back to jail for a long time or if we could do anything to keep him out of prison. They asked my mother to pick him up and that we could go home. We were astonished because being caught with a firearm had no chances of release. However, as my mother got into the deep, she found him with two detectives. They were set to explain a few things to my mother about my father's release conditions. To our surprise, the Southington detectives were assisting the Meriden police detectives with a federal case on the Diablos. They really thought having another insider informant that can easily infiltrate the gang to get any information would be worth its weight in gold. We were warned and told briefly about it. The police had us swear not to say anything about his release. Also, they explained that my father would be facing three to five years or imprisonment for the gun charge if he decided not to cooperate. The Southington police ultimately made a deal with detectives.

My father was now free from prison, and all he had to do was cooperate with

Southington and Meriden police as they assisted the federal departments. Though it might seem to be easy on the outside, it was way too dangerous. The Diablos were sheer beasts. They had a network that the police could not even think of. They were widespread, involved in much more than drug trafficking. They were brutal toward people in general. What more they could do to the traitor. It gave me shivers to even think what the police had got my father in. All because he was found with a gun given by that cab driver.

I began to analyze and realized that my father was set up. The gun was originated from the police as a boomerang tactic. The cops wanted to rope in the felon on trumped-up charges to use them as a bargaining tool for the Diablos' narcotics investigation. Consequently, using my father as an informant to *"stay out of trouble."* It was way deeper than we had thought of — the police were playing it smart with my father. They knew my father had been a very involved member of the gang and a friend to Jackie Baltas. Also, he was living out of the town and could easily infiltrate the gang. We could not believe he was actually doing this.

At this time, I wished for a miracle. A miracle that could save us all from all the mess that was going on in our lives. I desperately craved to have normal days back. When we all were happy, my dad would spend time with us carefree, and there was no fear. If only I could, I would.

My father's relapsing sent him to a path of least resistance as the police watched and knew him as the weak link to lead them to the gang. They made the most of his weakness and would threaten my father with jail so that he would comply. He would sit with us and tell us how much he loved us. He repeatedly said he did not want to do this because my father somehow knew the outcome, but he had no choice.

Chapter 4
Working as an
Informer or
Undercover Agent

My father had now begun his short journey of a mission to get these annoying cops off his back. I say a short journey because I can literally count the days when my father agreed to this deal to when he was found hanging inside his closet in Florida. These sly detectives would partake with him in the drug trafficking deals to gather intelligence against the Diablos and tell lies to my father. Like they would hand out high hopes saying they have got my father's back and that if he complies, they will save him from any further imprisonment and get him out of all this mess. They allowed my father to continue where he left off his rehabilitation in the streets.

However, immediately after then, my father began going back to his other mistress. He interacted with this lady whore friend he was seeing from up the street and Diablo biker club gang members for most of his drugs, including cocaine, heroin, and pills.

At this point, my father would do anything for his quest. He was trying many different practices, from breathing techniques to deep relaxation to studying the Bible and whatnot. My father knew his time was near, and he tried to strategize and plan an abrupt ending. He became more psychotic as the drugs hit well and his responsibilities to the detectives left our home time very scary. Only late at night or very early in the morning was the time when we could have a bit of peace in our conversations. I could see that a part of him began to hold onto us a little tighter, and I felt good about it. But he was still battling the raw urge to hit the streets, and he actually had to without any sobriety about him, and even though my father tried to be somewhat nicer, knowing he was in the deep mire, but that lasted a day or so.

The utter emotional agony of looking at his family, knowing that we all were going through hell described as the police, a biker gang, his insanely crazy habits, and that too him being the number one person in my life. My father was under immense pressure after signing this deal with the detectives, and he was so angry with the police but acted as if he was very thankful to them.

He began to act even more wired and engaged in stealing more than ever. Even the kids in the neighborhood had learned that he was stealing, and word started to get around really quick. This time he was also interested in pilfers and would even walk off with things that apparently would not mean anything for a person who had been dealing in grand larceny. First, he sold my mother's camper. Then one day, he went into my best friend Ronnie's house to check up on me as we lived in an apartment complex. He knocked, went in, and asked to use the bathroom for 10 minutes. Later Ronnie came over and told me all his mother's medication was missing from the bathroom medicine cabinet, and nobody else was in there except for my father. We really could not understand why my father was acting this strange.

The fights between my parents did not cease. She would make him go through hell every day, asking him how he planned on getting out of this situation and what was going on in his mind. This arguing did not help matters at all, and neither did the police, who supposedly had my father's back. I also believe one of the Southington detectives had taken my mother out to "talk to her" because she would never give up any information on the Diablos, even today. My father felt she was unfaithful and possibly sleeping or having sexual relations with that detective briefly, maybe a time or two. My father was so involved and headstrong that he almost felt invincible. There was this time when the Southington police came over, and my father told them to fuck off with themselves, and he fought with the two of them so hard, it ultimately took six officers to subdue him. He then explained that he was working as an informant, and they eventually cooled things down and walked off, embarrassed. My father seemed to be getting away with this title quite a bit at that time. My father became very outspoken at this point. He was snapping on some of the gangsters at the apartment complex. Often, he would make this guy, Tawn, run inside his girlfriend's house and hide in the bathroom like a little wuss for talking crap to him.

In terms of drugs, while my dad was working as an informant for the Southington and Meriden police detectives, he was told that he had to stay clean and could only use them in an emergency. For example, if he had to show up at any meetings of investigations with the clubhouse in Meriden. He was supposed to return to the Veteran outpatient program and receive his benzodiazepines and other medications for bipolar disorder and drug addictions. However, my father stayed extra high almost all the time. Not only did he have his Veteran's hospital medicines being overdosed, but he was also able to legally buy hard street narcotics from the biker gang under police supervision, and this was all taped and recorded for evidence

45

against the Diablos.

The hospital repeatedly asked him to be an outpatient after the inpatient program, and he was so reluctant about it because he had so many other things going on in his mind. Once, I remember while he was an inpatient, I visited him during his 2-day detox and treatment. He shared with me that he had seen a man writing on the chalkboard while he was asleep, and when he woke up, the chalkboard was filled front and back. I do not remember what my father told me the man had written. I think he said the Bible. I do not remember that very distinctively. In addition, he felt as if he did not have the time, and there were many more important things to deal with and prioritize because his days were numbered, and he wanted to make the most of his time left. Moreover, if he did not complete his tasks with the detectives, he would be charged with an offense for having a .38 special and violence with my mother. So, my father was only impatient.

Amidst my father's addiction to drugs and abuse of benzodiazepines, my father was constantly working for the detectives. He hit the streets so fast it was the very next day of the gun incident. Within days of him being caught with the firearm, he was being wired up for audio surveillance. He was taken to remote locations for the cabbie to bring him into Meriden, where my father would meet with detectives at Hubbard Park to relay orders and ask questions. Basically, they would tell my father what to ask, buy, demand from the Diablos biker gang. This occurred mostly in Meriden, in concurrence with the Southington police detectives because the clubhouse was in Meriden. He met with other undercovers to go into either dope spots, drug houses, or the Diablos clubhouse, wherever they might have been at the time.

At this time during the day, while my mother was at work, the detectives, usually Bruce Boislard from Southington PD, would pick my father up and bring him to Meriden. The detectives would show up in unmarked vehicles to pick my father up so they could bring him to collect information. Sometimes he would buy drugs, and at times he would only listen to business dealings and get them on record for the police. My father would then be brought to Wallingford or Southington's police department to debrief. This only happened successfully a few times. After that, the Diablos were smarter and started to sense that my father was acting funny.

At the same time, my father was having a very hard time getting high and keeping the elephant in the room. He was an actual narc, signed and sealed. A few weeks into the keep and out of jail routine, my father started acting very weird. Instead of all the heroin he did before, he was zippy because they switched his drug to cocaine, but I cannot confirm that because I was too young to sense that for sure. At that time, I did not know that my father had stolen my mother's 40' camper and sold that to act as if he was cool with the gang, and he was not busted by the police either. I mean, all he had to do was steal, tell the gang someone snitched and then act like it was not him. In the end, nobody gets caught, and my father served no prison time for being a felon with a firearm. He probably did this because he wanted to act normal for the gang.

The detectives would also talk to my mom and me, telling us that my father was doing the right thing and just trying to keep himself out of trouble. But after a few days went by, maybe a week or so, we started getting weird calls from the detectives talking to my mom about putting our family in protective custody if we needed it and how my father was to turn over all recordings. My father had days and weeks of recordings and interactions between the police, himself, and gang members. My father even purchased an extra recorder for recording the police conversations about having him record the Diablos biker gang. He told us that more than likely incriminating evidence was recorded against the biker gang and the corrupt police. He would tell the police over the phone that he had evidence against them to make them scared or go away. But I think my father discovered at this point that the local detective police case was actually ordered from a federal case against the Diablos, and it was much larger than my father suspected; it was not a situation to be put in and nor able to be stopped. So, you have to understand what the police department allowed- trafficking hundreds of thousands of dollars in narcotics — way beyond our imagination.

My dad decided to keep some recordings and say fuck the police. The police tried roughing him up a few times because he no longer wanted to comply. We knew this was not good. My father ended up wounded in the ER with an arm fracture, I believe. So my dad was lit. He told me he was not working with these lying pigs anymore, and he meant the police as they would get him killed.

Quite frankly, my father was strung out and did not want the repercussions. He just wanted out of the audio surveillance detectives' rides led by the police control. We were so scared as my father told me he might lose his life, but he loved us. My mother did not need this. She did not deserve to be hurt over and over again. My father said he had to make the inevitable right, fix his rattling, and not be sorry about the cops' cases against a gang he was not an official part of. My father no longer wanted to serve the ties. My father was digging his own grave, I believe the police and gang knew this, and my father was meant to be a sacrifice to strengthen their bonds.

When my father realized the police would do nothing to protect him in any case, he planned the other way out. Yes, my father decided to seek help from Jackie Baltas, the founder and leader of the Diablos and his very own friend. His paranoia was at an all-time high. I mean, the Diablos biker gang is a one-percenter gang that is well-known coast to coast from California to Connecticut, Florida to Maine, a very well-known motor club gang. One afternoon, my father looked dead straight in my eyes and said that he loved my mother and me so much and that he wanted to do something to keep us safe. He said he was taking me for a meeting with Jackie, and I agreed.

"Where are we going to meet him?" I asked him. *"The clubhouse?"*

"No, we are going to meet him in public, so he could not do anything. The place would be filled with people and vendors outside, and it will be easier to discuss current matters." He further added, *"He would not meet in public, but I told him it is extremely urgent, and I need to meet him now, so he agreed."*

We went to downtown Southington, the Apple harvest festival, a very crowded public place to meet him. My father had decided to tell him that the police had information against him and his gang, and they were planning on something big to charge them with a strong case against the hard drugs and all other things they were engaged in. It was a fine afternoon, and I still remember the day very distinctively. I was only fifteen at that time, but the anxiety and the fear on my father's face are something that I could never forget. He was so eager to get out of this. He wanted to end all this and move on with a normal life.

"The police has got recordings against you. They have used people to get into your gang, let transactions of narcotics and theft of vehicles go on only to build the case they needed against the gang and organization," my father told him.

"So, what next?" he asked.

Jackie was a huge, fat biker man, chain wallet and long beard, yeah scary crap he was.

"I need your help, and I want you to protect my family, and at the same time, I want to make sure that there would not be collateral damage to me, my sisters or my

wife, his mother," replied my father.

"Yeah, look, man, huh, there is nothing I can do for you; nothing at all. Do you get me?"

I could see the despair and the helplessness on my father's face. Jackie was the last option my father could go for, that too risking his deal with the police and getting himself in real danger. Because if the police got to know that my father tried to double-cross them, they could do anything and everything to have him meet his Creator. Literally anything. There was sheer silence for a few seconds while my father was frozen, and Jackie seemed to be so relaxed even after knowing that the police were planning out a trap for them.

My father tried insisting, but a straight denial was plastered on Jackie's face.

"Hey, listen," he added. *"We do not touch women and children, okay? So, you can*

be relaxed for your wife, kid, and your girls from our side. I can't say anything else."

He was busy eating his chili dogs, and my father and I left the Apple harvest festival. I was crying and asked my father what that was for? He explained that he had told the police about the Diablos, and he had also told the Diablos (Jackie) about the police. He expected it to be a win-win situation, but things do not always turn out to be the way we expect them. When Jackie said there was nothing he could do for him, we knew he meant that my father would be killed anytime soon. It could be by the party. My father had suddenly grabbed me up and said we had to leave. He sped home so fast in a tizzy, frantic manner. My mother scolded him for playing both sides and how he might have to continue working with the police. She was scared, and so was I. My father regretted believing the cops and infiltrating the gang, and cheating on Jackie. He regretted being used as a narc and a handler and playing both sides, penetrating a gang he befriended 20 years before he knew my mother.

The call came in, and they said they needed my father's testimony immediately for the case, and the raid of the Diablos clubhouse was going down. We were shattered. They said that if he did not comply, he would have to face prison, but my father decided to ditch and split up.

Chapter 5
Escaping to Florida

A lot was going on in my father's mind. My father was in serious trouble now that he had decided not to comply with the detectives and had a meeting with Jackie, informing him about the detectives' moves. He knew that the Diablos could do anything, even kill him, and the police could arrest him easily because he had now broken the deal. My mother and I were extremely worried because of his decision, and my mother tried to convince him to stick to the deal and save himself but my father, I believe, had something even more prominent on his mind. My mother tried to initiate a conversation with my father to ask him what he would do next, but he refrained from talking.

DIABLOS: MURDER OR SUICIDE?

The next day, my father visited home. I am unsure whom he was with. I think he was tying up loose ends there too. My father kept to the door only and did not want to come in. It was strange, and he acted weird. My father told me that he was leaving for a while until things cool down and that he would only be gone for a few weeks. He said he needed to lay low, but I was confused and thought maybe he was going to some safe house to be there for some time. Initially, he said he was going to see some family in Florida, but he left so quickly that I could not process what had happened. I realized that my father should have never taken this deal or any deal with the police. Because no one knew for sure how deep this rabbit hole would go.

My father had family from his mother's married side in Florida too. He actually had a lot of family in Florida. They may have assisted him with an address, some food, and a place to stay. It was known that my father had stayed at a motel named Heritage Inn in Florida. I also believe the narcotics were being trafficked from Florida, and my father had known this, to be sure. I believed that gang members of various organizations were trafficking drugs, including cocaine and heroin. Florida was one honey hole and landing strips with flights private in from the Dominican Republic. I cannot confirm this all from a fifteen-year-old's perspective, but I have had many curiosities. One thought was that the detectives from Florida were allowing the trafficking of narcotics to occur. And unknowingly, the Diablos and my father led the federal investigators to where the narcotics were being derived from.

My father left from Southington, Connecticut, to Port St. Lucy, Florida. I believe he had left with a girl he found in Meriden, possibly from the biker gang he had a relationship with. My father was trying to allow things to cool down. Shortly after my father left Connecticut and flew to Florida, the police detectives from Connecticut were calling and looking to talk to him. I was given a cell phone and pager back in the nineties when he flew to Florida, and the only call conversation was the detectives questioning me if my father said where he was going. I answered no and asked them to fuck off. They said my father could be in a lot of trouble. But somehow, I think they knew Florida was a good place for my father not to come back home. It felt like they had this going on in their minds: *If there is a killing to do, just have it done there in Florida; a lot of things will be quiet and go away smoothly.*

My father called when he reached

Florida and told my mother that he stopped in a VA to get some medications and had been an inpatient at a VA hospital when he left for Florida. He went in for maybe a day or two only. My father was staying at his mother's property in a trailer they had outside the home from Florida. My father was hiding out, but he did tell people he thought he could trust why he was hiding for snitching, working with police audio recording and surveillance on the Diablos motorcycle gang back up north.

It had been only a few days when the detectives began calling to harass my mom, saying if my father did not come back to testify, he would go to prison. She was threatened to produce any information she might have regarding the Diablos or my father. The police asked my mother if she could record any calls from my father. I believe one or two detectives came to our apartment at that time and assisted my mother in operating the recording device. The detectives told my mother that if the recorded tapes that had information about the Diablos were not recovered from my father and given to them, she would go to prison too. The detectives asked my mother that if there was even a little information about where my father was, then she was supposed to inform them and not withhold. They wanted him to return, or he would face charges. But the fact was that he would have to face charges anyway because the police knew that he had leaked the information and that there were informants involved with the Diablos who were constantly tapping their deals via audio surveillance for the police department of Southington and Meriden. But the really obvious thing was to look left while talking right, meaning threaten with simple and scary charges while homicide was taking place.

DIABLOS: MURDER OR SUICIDE?

The detectives contacted my mother several times, and they seemed to have a lot of questions for her. Definitely, the detectives were tying up any loose ends, but my mother had no answers to any of those questions. They tried taking us in confidence because we were the key for them to get to my father. One of them, I do remember, was a detective from Southington named Bruce. In confidence, he had told me everything would be okay, but things only got worse. The police were just making bogus promises and false assurances that they could save my father and had his back if he came back and provided them with all the recordings.

The detectives had one recording where the Diablos threatened to kill a law officer. Therefore, we were also offered witness protection because they believed that officer in question was my dad. They could also use this recording against the Diablos after murdering my father. To be honest, the detectives were not concerned about our lives but only the recordings and my father's testimony against the Diablos.

They were even more conscious now because I told detective Bruce about the meeting with Jackie in Southington at the Apple Harvest. The case was crucial to the police department, and they had been working on this extensively. They wanted to earn a name when my father made all the effort. They had an idea that with my father, the recording could be gone too. I was only fifteen at the time and could not clearly understand all these things, so I cannot be sure of it. My mother refused to take the protection because she felt we would be okay with my father away. She had a few phone conversations with my father when he called from Florida during this time. He said that he had found a veterans' hospital for medications and a hotel to stay. I think he was with that young lady biker chick girlfriend with whom he had left Southington, Connecticut.

At first, my father thought he could run to Florida because he had half-brothers, brothers, sisters, mom, some people, and a place to stay. I also believe that ultimately my father thought he could have us come to Florida, but time did not allow us that. I also believe things in Florida happened too fast, and between time and drugs, the few days or weeks that my father was in Florida were clouded by guidance from whoever was going to kill him, even if it was himself.

My mother would talk to my father on the phone and would ask him about his safety and still try to convince him to get back and comply with the police for the sake of his life. But he no longer had anything to do with it, or at least that seems to be what he thought.

DIABLOS: MURDER OR SUICIDE?

My mother tried her best to convince my father in some way or the other, but he was adamant not to come back. My father came forward to the gang and met Jackie at the Apple Harvest to try to make things right, and he promised he would withhold the recordings the detectives made him record. He said he would not testify against their gang, and he wanted to be a man of his words.

Most conversations were between my father and mother and my mother and the detectives. I only talked to my father once after he stormed off to Florida for what reason, I could only suppose at that time. But I could sense that he did not go to meet family there. So, I suppose he bugged out, and I know how scared he was, but the way the information was being relayed, I felt that this horrible phase would end soon, and he would also be saved from going to jail. But it was too soon to conclude anything of this sort because I also believe that it is possible that my father was there because of some drug trafficking matter, as Florida was one of the spots where drugs would land. As far as my father's involvement with narcotics is concerned, he could never be out of trouble somehow or the other.

While my mother and father were still in contact through phone calls, I remember the only time when I had talked to my father. I did not know it would be the last time my father and I would talk. The man I loved the most and could not imagine my life without was far and distanced from me, and I felt helpless. I walked into the living room, and my mother was on the phone with my father. It was around 3 in the afternoon. She asked me to get on the phone and speak to my dad, so I did. I asked him how he was and what was up. I told him that I loved him and missed him a lot. I inquired, *"When is this going to be over?"*

He said he could not tell if everything was alright. There were voices in the background. He said that I needed to be very strong and brave. He wanted me to take care of my mother, and I said that I would. I was so broken at this point that all I wanted was for him to come back and hold my mother and me in his arms and start anew. I was just a kid, and it had already been too much for me. I asked him when he would return home and inquired what he was doing to get back home; I asked if he was coming home. And why did he leave at the last moment? He seemed very scared and said to me he might not see me again, and I didn't understand what that meant, maybe I could have saved him? I gave the phone back to my mother and screamed at her to ask him to bring his fucking self back. I could not imagine losing him ever.

DIABLOS: MURDER OR SUICIDE?

Late in the night, about 2 am, my mother's phone rang. She answered with greetings, and then she started wailing, *"Michael, Michael, they got him, your father."* I asked, *"What?"* and she screamed, *"HE'S DEAD, HE'S DEAD; they got your father; he's dead, Michael."* My life was over.

Chapter 6
Suicide or Murder?

*"The ties of my father with Jackie will now
be forever served as I long for answers that
I never got."*

My mother knew this was coming,
whether it was from the police's side or the
Diablos' side. I remember my mother
screaming at him one day, asking him to get
his life straight and have mercy on himself
and us. I just could not believe that the man I
loved the most and the man I am forever
obliged to, committed suicide. Or should I
rather say he has been murdered?

My dad was not a coward. He would
look straight into one's eye and even tell the
police to fuck off. I know my father, and I can
confidently say that he would never commit

71

suicide. All this time, he was being set up to be eventually killed. Even though I was just fifteen at that time and there were multiple things I did not understand or could tell if they were the way they seemed to be, but one thing I can be sure of is that the police are lying. They had all played very well with my father and made the most of him. They did not care about his life when what they had promised him was his life in return for the deal. I wonder how the police can be so pathetic and how they can be so incompetent to not get one thing right for my father?

Nothing was ever communicated to us clearly by the police about my father's death except for a few statements. No documents were shared about his case. All that I got to know was either because I found it on my own or because I began to be a pain in their ass. So, they had to hand over something to me to shut my mouth. From that, I am sure they had kept a lot from my mother and me, and all that is kept from us is the actual truth. After a few weeks of my father flying to Florida, the actual purpose of which is still unknown, he was found hanging in the closet of the Heritage Inn in Stuart, Florida, where he was staying. However, I have some idea as to why he flew to Florida; either to let matters cool down or to visit his family there. Another possible reason could be because he knew that the major trafficking of the drug was being originated from Florida, and he wanted to unveil that.

He left with this girl who was supposedly a member of the Diablos. I believe she was the one to set him up for the kill, all while keeping him high and away from his family with drugs, sex, and promises of safety, like let's lay low after what you just did. My father was losing his mind. How could he have snitched on his best friend

DIABLOS: MURDER OR SUICIDE?

Jackie Baltas, the founder of the Diablos biker gang? Out of all people, what a fucking idiot he said he was, and though I am not fond of the gang, I can say that if my father had stayed faithful to him, he might have saved him.

We knew that he was in Florida, but where exactly, we do not know. I believe the detectives knew where in Florida he was. At this time, there were plenty of interactions of this Diablos case, and it went down in a big way that we were not aware of. When I was told he was strangulated to death with his very own belt and was found hanging in a closet where the hotel room door was open that alerted the police, I found it very fishy. Wasn't he supposed to be hiding out in safety as he had just recorded the leader and gang members of the Diablos? Was not he supposed to be caring about saving his life because he had with him full interactions tapped about all the Diablos' dealings? Who did they want dead, what drugs were they trafficking from whom? What police were involved, and if anyone from the police was or was not part of it? My dad recorded it all. Do the police think my dad was a fool to leave the door open while he attempted suicide? Or do the police think we are fools to believe what they say to us? Was it easy for them to shut the case saying he simply committed suicide without even investigating it? Didn't the person who had put his life at stake for their deal deserve to receive justice?

All they could do was just hand over some sympathies. I remember this interaction with detective Bruce Boislard who said that my father was a good man and did not deserve this. Yes, he did not deserve this at all and now deserves justice that you fail to give him. I would never ever believe in the cops because they were of no help at all.

75

Instead, they would threaten. I became so fearful that upon seeing their cars, I would run and hide. I even sought help from detective Pakonis in Florida, who worked on my father's case and voiced my opinions before him. But he screamed at me and threatened that he would drag me to court. I was only fifteen years, so I got afraid, and my heart would palpitate. Later, he said he would help me, but he would need the original reports that were with the Southington police. I struggled and ordered a report from the medical examiner, but detective Pakonis failed to identify with me what it actually meant for my father to be an informant.

When in Florida, I believe my father may have uncovered the trafficking of cocaine from Florida to Connecticut. The people he thought would protect him were not with him to keep him safe, but instead, they set him up to be killed. For example, the girl with whom he left from Meriden disappeared from the hotel, and the medical examiner's report does not state her name. I remember the last time I talked to my father over the phone. There were a lot of voices in the background. When I asked him what was up and what was wrong, he insisted he could not tell. The voices in the background grew louder. Finally, he said he loved me and asked me to tell my mother and my sisters that he loved them so much. I believe he was in serious trouble, and the people in the background were constantly leading him. Why was there no record of these people visiting him there? Why would the police not investigate this?

I recently spoke to an Italian half-brother of my father; he asked me, *"How did it happen; in the shower?"* His question floored me, so I told him that was not the case and inquired why he would say that? *"I thought,"* he said. So, I interrupted Mr. Joe Dominello and informed him that my father was found in a motel closet in Florida because that is what the police informed me. He said, *"Oh, the closet. yeah."*

Now, I have the medical examiner's report that I had ordered, but he does not, and the report states that it appears to be that the first suicide attempt was in the shower or bathroom. However, the detective who was there on the first scene told me that he responded to a call for an open door at the motel that seemed unusual. Upon checking in the room, he found my father dead hanging in the closet. I could not process how Mr. Joe Dominello would even think of this. So, during the conversation, I questioned him if he was aware of anything related to the drugs, and he said yes because he had known the detective who was the first to find my father dead. He further added that Detective

DIABLOS: MURDER OR SUICIDE?

Pakonis contacted him (someone he claims to know) and told him that his half-brother (my father) had committed suicide and was found dead after doing crack with his half-sister. I said, *"Wow, that is interesting."* Now Detective Pakonis repeatedly told me that he does not know my father, which I suspect because if not, how could he know that it was Joe Dominello's half-brother who was found dead and called him to inform?

The question arises: How would Joe know about the tub things because he does not have the medical examiner's report? How did he know the detective, and is he also a part of the drug triangle? There was so much going on in my mind, so many questions whose answers I did not have. And not to mention I have the right to a young man's opinion. Mr. Joe Dominello also grew up on Grove Street in Meriden, two houses down from the Diablos clubhouse, so did Mr.

DIABLOS: MURDER OR SUICIDE?

Dominello know the Diablos? Of course, yes, he did. I asked if he knew any more about the narcotics or my father's death, but he just advised me to speak to his sister and my father's half-sister. So, my father was found to have connections in Stuart, Florida, yet my mother and I were told he was hiding out in port St. Lucy, Florida. Again, the police had lied. I believe my father had way too much info on the way to too many people.

I happened to talk to Susan Dominello a few days back, and she told me that she did go to the motel but only to rent a room for my father and his girlfriend. According to her, my father met at the psychiatric hospital's outpatient facility. She said she left from there immediately after them because she was not allowed to meet my father or even talk to him. But if I compare the statements of Susan and the detective information, they are contradictory. As per the detective story, she was there with my father, but she says she dropped them and went away. There is even more to this story that her brothers and father are aware of but hiding from me.

When I focused on the address on my father's examiner's report, to my amazement, it was of Florida's, and this guy named Robert Dominello, whom I have hardly met once or twice in my life, was listed as the next of kin of my father's house. My question is, how did the detective know my dad's address to be Robert Dominello's address because my father lived in Connecticut, and he had Connecticut's driving license. I researched the address and found that it was listed as this guy's former-owned property. So, what was going on here? Did they know the Diablos and detective enough to have covered up my father's death? I tried to speculate the detective, but Mr. Dominello threatened me.

He began to scream at me and demanded an apology from me when I was the one who had lost his father to a hanging or now what Mr. Dominello says to a bathroom tub? I am now convinced that the police are involved and have lied to me and portrayed my father's murder as a suicide, so they do not have to investigate because my father was an informant. I believe what Mr. Joe Dominello says is the truth that my father was found in the tub. Probably he was strangulated in the bathroom after being uncontrollably high from some heroin cocktail made by the crack-smoking girlfriend and gang who were with him, whose voices I heard on the phone.

My father's half-brothers and sister knew this gang well, even today. However, they have never reached out to me. The half-brother also claimed to know the detective that found my father and solely determined his death as suicide and has threatened me.

Apparently, my father's half-brother made me feel that his side of the family acted as if they were in good faith and would keep my father safe. But from what my mother tells me, I know that my father's stepdad Robert Dominello did not like my father. He thought that my father was a bad person because he was doing a lot of narcotics along with his daughter. In a nutshell, my father's half-sister was involved in narcotics with my father and took care of drug trafficking in Florida. They also had found my father was snitching on Jackie.

Now were these family members actually the middlemen of my father's hanging? Because it is very suspicious that I am recently learning some of the unexpected connections from when my father was found dead. Also, my mother recently told me that before the medical examiner's report, she was informed the cause of death to be an overdose of narcotics and not a suicide death by hanging asphyxiation. So, something definitely happened to my father at the Heritage Inn in Stuart, Florida, in September of 1995, and there is an involvement of my father's other side of the family. Is it them who joined hands with Jackie and planned to get him to Florida and have him killed with the help of the police? I need to get an answer on my own because the police are useless, and their real intentions are unlawful. Is it really suicide or murder?

Chapter 7
Young Kid – An Investigator

My mind was stuck on a hanging body in the closet and certain key events — for example, a warm hug or a kiss from my father. I can still feel his touch, the gentle embracing that would make me feel assured and safe as a young kid. The times he showed up to the house with new convertibles, stolen cars. His crazy acts of stealing, even from neighbors, and his threats to people for their lives. All is summed up in that one moment of his demise.

Before the loss of my father, I was a young boy who seemed to be very smart, the knowing-too-much type. I was building my commodore 64, trying to make the internet happen. Video gaming and skateboarding were really cool to me. I was timid and probably the most softspoken or quiet boy there was.

But when I actually had to speak up, I was loud, and people listened to me. The day I got off the phone and found my father was killed, I knew right then that my life was about to change forever drastically.

It is so hard to describe the nineties, and the importance is his presence in our lives. I asked myself back then why no investigation was there. It didn't make sense how there could be none when a significant informant for the police was found dead, hanging, strangulated in the closet of a local motel. There should have been an investigation, and most other things that led to his death became irrelevant for me. So, I thought and reasoned from the mind of a child.

From day one, I sought only justice. I hungered for truth and thirsted for the blood of my father's murderer. We lived in Southington when my father started to cooperate with the police investigating the Diablos gang for death threats on an officer, trafficking of narcotics and stolen vehicles and motorcycles. He was taken from the Southington police department to the Wallingford police department to debrief information recorded on his wiretaps. This was done so the Diablos would not be able to track my father's police-related work activities.

I must have moved more than twenty times after my father was found dead, from Meriden to Wallingford, Connecticut to Florida to Wisconsin to Maine, and where not? You name a place in the US, and I have lived there. I was in constant motion, all for the sake of trying to find answers. I was in search of just one single Diablo's gang member who could point a finger to himself and say, "I did it," or that the police were involved.

The police were only bothered about getting their part right. They would be sarcastic at times, trying to act and show that they took matters on a lighter note, whereas I knew it would all end badly. Why would they think it was bad? For them, it was a matter of routine. I will never forget that one time when the detectives came over for my dad, one of them patted my head and said to me, *"You are going out with that girl, the one I see that in the picture, huh?"*

I said, *"Yes."*

He said to my father, *"He must have got a big thing,"* and began to laugh, trying to express the 90s humor. I did not really give a fuck what he said because neither did I give a fuck about who he was.

It was only a matter of weeks after my father's death in Stuart, Florida, that my mother and I moved back to Meriden - the city of the Diablos. She not only refused protective custody but somehow moved into a beautiful new condo with a garage. She also had a couple of part-time burly guys by her side named Kenny and Bear, a big guy with a fuzzy beard helping her. I think they were both bikers.

Then, I even found another guy on the couch one day whose name was Tom. I did not quite understand all this, but I tried to get along with it. At this time, I began to smoke weed to suppress the emotions deep within me and consequently began to feel absolutely numb. Smoking weed at 16 was mind-blowing, but I was able to do it and subdue almost anything. This fact alone made me highly shocked and confused.

DIABLOS: MURDER OR SUICIDE?

Initially, my mom did not say a whole lot about the situation. Instead, she cried and screamed that they had killed him. To be honest, it was just that one time. Afterward, she never really wanted to mention it ever again. Finally, she gathered herself up and became strong - cold, I would rather say. She had this quality in her, and she even kept my oldest sister hidden from everybody for forty years. We have just found out she had given birth to a baby girl ten years earlier and never told us.

The way I see things now is that my mom just does not want inherent involvement. Although we both know this Diablos case, it is unclear whether it was murder or suicide because my father could be as crazy as psychotic. My mother could not do it on her own, and my father was not there for her. I guess time for them went by fast, but for me, time stopped when he left.

DIABLOS: MURDER OR SUICIDE?

The police stopped calling once we moved because they understood that everything had come to an end with my father, and chasing us would yield them nothing but would be a mere waste of time. My mother had more friends now than she ever had. She frequently began to go to the clubs. I believe my aunt owned one bar called Chas' Place that my mother frequently visited in Meriden. The irony is that as much as she wanted my father to get out of this fuss and make things straight, she was never really afraid of the idea of how it would end.

After his death, she was not hesitant to say from time to time, *"He got what he was looking for."* It was, but only for a while. I believe my mother really wanted to know more about how my father was found. Firstly, she accepted the excuse that my father's half-brother called was an overdose from narcotics. But once she heard of the strangulation, she was past the event and refused to question it. My mother would rather obey the police than question them as I do. Unfortunately, my mother never told me anything more; even if she knew way more, I'd get way less, so I had to dig in the truth on my own. My mother may have secrets or think her kids know everything, but the truth is that honesty may not be for another.

As time passed, the hunger for the truth stayed, and as a young boy, I began to search for answers to all the questions that kept piercing my heart. I moved out of the home to see if I could investigate how my father died. The path was tough, but I had to walk down anyways. I was lost and at the same time in a constant fight and flight mode. It was like a tailspin into a life with no parents, and I leaned into many directions — first, a girlfriend who was way older than me whose name was Jennifer. I needed an escape, and she was only interested in sex.

Initially, I moved in with her in her parent's house. I was fifteen at that time, and she took care of me. My mother was working and was out most of the time. I was lost and needed someone to hold me together and keep from shattering. My mother knew that Jennifer was a good person, and perhaps it was the best thing for me at that time.

I became paranoid and grew even more aggressive. Even if I knew the answer, I would get it wrong. My entire concentration was on sex with this amazing woman and forgetting the fact that it had been a while since my father was dead.

Initially, my mother and I were told that he died because of an overdose, and that is it. No paperwork, no real explanation for so many years. I did everything from running away from home to living across the street in a third-floor apartment from the Diablos clubhouse to find answers. Although I did not investigate, I was running, hiding, and playing while in shock, amazed by the marijuana and sexual engagements I had at that time. I was sure that even if they did not kill him, they knew who did it.

My personality? It became like a wild animal and horrific, like a ghost in a sense that I felt limitless. And then these infamous streets where the gangs and drugs were, I hit them hard. I was looking for a killer or killers. I dropped out of high school to knock on doors and ask questions, hoping to get some other information.

I moved back to the Meriden area after some time of laying low with Jennifer. I met this cab driver named Billy. He was semi-retired, and I would smoke joints with him and a kid I met named Michael Johnson. Billy was cool, but once we went to pick up some weed, he pulled out a pistol to show me.

DIABLOS: MURDER OR SUICIDE?

I was already paranoid, so I ran outside the apartment to wait for a ride back home. People might wonder why I should hang out with this cab driver? I really needed to know what happened to my father; who else to ask besides a semi-retired city cab driver and a loud pipe saves lives anyways. Shirt, bandana, wearing a ponytail, and having a kid named Mike Johnson, I was trying to connect the dots with any information I could find related to my father's case from anyone. Amidst this all, after a few more years had passed, I promised my mom I would go back to school to get my diploma. She needed me to do that, but there were so many unanswered questions.

Many times, Michael told me that we would figure this out, and I believed him. He had a widespread network and knew everyone. He was well respected among the biker gangs and even hood gangs.

Unfortunately, Billy ended up moving to Florida, and Michael Johnson ended up getting stabbed to death in Bellows Falls, Vermont. Although I know he would have loved to help in asking questions and find how my father was killed, he already had a lot going on, so I did not want to be bothersome.

By this time, my investigations were coming up with a *Beware: Caution* sign. I was chased out of town for a bit by the gang members, where I picked up with a woman named Deborah Hilton. Her name, I will never forget. She, too, was much older than me. She had an ex-husband who was a biker. We spent months together trying to figure out who might have killed my father or who might know who killed my father. I have to admit I was still young and in my teens and was not much sure what to do with the information if I even got to know, but I still wanted to know anyways.

I remember working at a local Food Bag gas station, and I'll never forget when this lady named Laurie came up to me. She was older, and I knew she could get my mind off the obsession of knocking on the clubhouse doors. She slipped an oxycontin pill over the counter and said, *"Here, take this and meet me outside after you're out of work."* I was melting, and we did everything.

I told Laurie I really wanted to find out what happened to my dad, and she said she could help me. She added she knew the Diablo's very well and warned me not to fuck with them. *"Who are you? Stupid?"* she said. We dated for a while, but she was older and into a lot of things as far as the streets and even beyond that. Laurie ended up having a child with a current Diablo member.

Although Laurie loved me very much, she never wanted to see me getting hurt. She believed that if the Diablos could have my father killed, they could have also had the matter brushed under the carpet. Laurie never wanted to tell me what she may have known, but she always wanted to console me and tell me not to worry and that everything would be alright. A few times, she said the Diablos may have killed him, but she also said that I would be dumb and stupid to find out. Because even if I did, what good would it do to me, or what would I do with the information? Anyway, it's not like someone is going to come up to me and say, *"Yeah, I killed your father, hang me the way I hanged him."*

While my age was to be in my parent's house and be raised up well, when I needed comfort and home and family, I was out on the streets. I faced near-death experiences trying to find answers to the greatest loss of my life.

DIABLOS: MURDER OR SUICIDE?

I planned on going in the clubhouse to the Diablos with a reason to buy some cocaine. Once I thought I could tell them who I was, they might feel like sharing the real story with me, but I was so dumb for even thinking that way. I was given cocaine soaked in gasoline, and I almost died for asking about my father's death. Laurie took me in until I was recovered from that near-death experience and told me, for real, to leave it alone.

Years passed by, and I would mostly roam the streets with a local Latin gang. I stayed with them at various hotels with the promises of getting someone to screech about my father's demise and utter nothing but the truth. Although every time I met someone who would share something about the case with me, even though it was what I already knew, I would feel I was a little more successful than before. I rarely felt that I had facts regarding the case except when people said, *"I do not agree it was a suicide"* or *"They definitely had him killed."* And I would be like, *"Okay! but who?"*

While being in Meriden, not far from the Diablos clubhouse, one afternoon, I built up the courage to go knock at the front door of the house that was the actual house of the club. It was the central place of all the activities, while the clubhouse was the hangout place. I knocked nice and heavy, and there came this bearded fellow. I think his name was Shane or Shawn; I am not sure.

I said, *"Hey,"* and he replied that he could not help me right now. I told him, *"You might probably know why I am here."*

"It is about my father," I informed him. He said, *"Yeah, I know."*

I replied, *"Okay, but what happened?"*

"I just took one of these," he said. He

had a patch on his chest; I asked him what that was. The only response he offered me was, *"Liquid morphine."* Then, he began to nod while sitting on a chair with no shirt and a body full of tattoos. While I watched him, I asked if he was okay, and he said, *"Yeah."* Something didn't feel right about the whole thing, and I ran out of that house soon after.

I stayed low-key, networking from home, and tried to begin a new life for my girlfriend of the time and me. I was always too involved in finding closure for my father's death.

During all this time, I was tough. I always had more fire with an attitude of 'fuck you' while looking dead straight in your eyes. In fact, I was all fired up, adrenalized. I was so smooth before I asked to be around the local gangs or biker gangs. I started slanging weed.

Once, this coke dealer who was a

member of the Diablos came in and waved a big rock around. *"A coke,"* he said. No one said anything; the quarter pound of weed got sold, and everyone left. The point is, it happened in a basement, and I was there too. I did not get caught or killed, and I felt like a man for at least telling my story there.

A few years later, I met this Latin gang member who was famous by the name *fa$e*. He assured me that my father was killed and that he could protect me as I tried to find out who might be the murderer. By this point, the police were no more into us, and the Diablos clubhouse was raided. Some very bad people went to jail for the things my father was informed about. I still had no idea about the cause of the death of my father. However, by spending time with gangs, I learned how they functioned in the city streets, how the streets were kept, and by whom. They never let me get too close to it.

DIABLOS: MURDER OR SUICIDE?

It was like a game, if you know what I mean.

I wound up staying in the apartment across the street from the Diablos clubhouse on the third floor. Although some of the gang members got locked up, not all, this was a vast and organized crime syndicate. I tried some harder street drugs thinking that would get me close to the club, but they knew who I was. If it was not for my partner ice brother *fa$e*, I would have probably been dead too.

Chapter 8
A Fight for Justice

It has been years since the death of my father; still, it seems as if it was the past week when my father came home and pointed a gun toward my mother and as if it was just the other day when he knocked on the door saying, *"I am flying off to Florida,"* hoping that life will settle once he comes back. Then, we all will walk out of that night into the bright day. But who knew the life of that little boy would be condemned to darkness as the sun of his life would be hanged in the closet.

Others may forget his death, the police, the Diablos, or my mother, who accepted everything as it is. But for me, this can never fade, and neither do I want this. At least not until I have won the fight for justice.

I wonder how the police can be so cold and not care about the person who gave up his life while helping them uncover the gang they had been hunting for years.

For years, I kept searching and wondering why the police would not investigate my father's case, and they made us believe that he had died of asphyxiation. I knew that the police were cruel, but I did not think they were liars, cheaters, and hypocrites, and so were the detectives. Later, I also learned how the Pathologist of my father's case, Frederick P Hobin, the 23rd District Medical Examiner in South Florida, was involved in a high-profile case simultaneously. Not to anyone's amazement, it may be that he had exchanged the findings of my father's case with another due to pressure from the cops. Because the same medical examiner in 2010 became the limelight for his controversial statements in respect to the medical report of Michelle O'Connell, who was forged. Michelle was allegedly shot dead by the service weapon belonging to her live-in boyfriend. Frederick changed his statement thrice from murder to suicide (though she was concluded to be shot by someone else) due to pressure from deputy Sheriff David Shoar and eventually declared it to be a homicide.

In the end, Michelle O'Connell received justice as later the truth was revealed, and Dr. Hobins was suspended for an undetermined period for hiding his amended opinion that Ms. O'Connell had been shot dead by someone else at home. He was also asked to be reprimanded for letting people view autopsy photographs of Ms. O'Connell without her family's permission. But my father still hasn't received justice. No wonder it is because we were laypeople with no power, and I was the only child. The cops of my father's case may have pressured him to change his verdict on the report and declare it to be suicide and hide the real homicide story. But I am trying to get the medical examiner to overturn the original opinion from suicide to homicide through the form, 'DH434A', affidavit of the medical amendment.

It boiled my blood when I saw the Facebook page of detective Pakonis flaunting pontoon planes to the Dominican Republic. I also said to him that the connection I had from the Dominic Republic, who was selling cocaine and crack cocaine told me that the drug trafficking was originating from there and traveling to Florida then up toward Connecticut. I wonder how he can make so much money as to flaunt it this way. After the Diablos were ultimately exposed to drug trafficking and, amongst other charges, the Southington police received a brand-new police department across town. All this happened after a few months of my father being found dead. The two might not be related, but out of curiosity, one may never know, and the way the police have treated my father, I could believe anything of this sort.

They even put out a story on Netflix "True Detectives" called operation Diablos. I called the feds in this matter, and when they returned, my call was only to listen to their episode, which said nobody lost their lives in the entire expedition. I mean, what a way to cover up the death of the man who was pressurized and forced to turn against his one best friend, Jackie, who happened to be a gang leader.

I was young before and did not have enough sense in which direction to go, so I did what was reasonable from the mind of a teen. I ended moving out to Wisconsin to getaway after a few years of my father's death. But I swore I would not give up on his life ever. I was making more well-thought-out calls to police or investigators to seek information. I hung around with gangs in the streets to make contacts that could provide me with any lead. I engaged in drugs to establish physical proximity with the Diablos. It was not until my mid-twenties that I first found out that I could get the medical examiner's report instead of just wandering here and there to know at least what had happened to my father. However, they were without the photographs when I got the reports because they said they could not release them to me as my mother is still alive. But I wonder why after all, I am his only son.

I was unfamiliar with legal matters and was not smart enough to know what to do with any information I had. Therefore, when I finally got the medical examiner's report, I contacted detective Bill Pakonis for the first time because he was the first officer on the death scene of my father. I began trying to process what happened better and thought he would be of great help. I got his name from the medical report, and I googled his number and looked for him on Facebook. But I still did not know the other side of my father's family, and my mother would rarely speak of them. I then focused on the address written and noticed that it was Florida's and that his death was declared a suicide. He asked me to get the original police report so he could help me in some way. Smart fucking cop knew that the records would not be there anymore as Florida's record had been mysteriously purged after the suicide label was given to my father's death.

They were able to erase all police records having no active case, although a homicide could be open for over 85 years in the state of Florida, but not suicide.

Therefore, they did not investigate, and the case was closed, saying it was a matter of mere suicide. Suicide? Why would my father even commit suicide in the first place? I know that he did not; instead, they made it look like a suicide so they could get rid of this entire matter. I believe detective Pakonis was part of this because he was aware that even if I tried, I would not get the record. After all, the Florida police department at the time may have had no prior knowledge of my father's death.

When I called him and told him that I felt my father's death was suspicious and that how my father was an active informant working with local and federal agents in Southington and Meriden, Connecticut, he said he was sorry and told me he was the officer there. I further added that I saw on his Facebook profile that he flies pontoon planes, to which he consented. However, when I made a smart remark saying, *"Is that how all this narco-trafficking is going on and the one snitch happens to supposedly commit suicide."* I further mentioned to him that I had heard how he is retired and owns a private firm of two persons called quiet investigations out of Florida, making six figures.

The phone call was dropped. I called again. I told him I was pissed because there was no investigation and that he did not know and was unsure. I told him how I was told that my father was killed in port St. Lucy. I am amazed that he did not correct me then and say that no your father was found in Stuart, Florida, at the Heritage Inn. I found that extremely strange.

A few more years went by, and I contacted former detective Pakonis several more times. I even called him when George Floyd died to let him know that I will never forget my father's death. I questioned him why he put Dominello's address on the report and how he got that information about the address. I asked him where my dad's wallet was and his license with Connecticut ID. That's when he told me a story. He found my father hanging in the closet by his belt and that my father was doing crack cocaine with Susan, his half-sister, and committed suicide. After that, I reached out to investigate the address and talked to Joe Dominello, and later reached out to Susan. Joe Dominello explained to me how he too had known the Diablos and grew up on Grove Street in Meriden at his mother's house next to Diablo's clubhouse. He told me that the Diablos are a very mean gang and would not hesitate to kill you.

Back then, Susan told me that after she dropped my father at the motel, she immediately left but recently got back to me after all these years and said she was there the night my father died and claims there were no drugs. However, her brother Joe says otherwise. He told me a few things in confidence about the drug abuse and trafficking that was going on in Florida, and my father was letting everyone know why he went to hide in Florida and that too with the Dominellos.

The question is, could my father trust the Dominellos who had such profound and well-seeded relationships with the city people? Detective Pakonis told me that he knew Joe Dominello and Joe told me Pakonis knew Susan and his father. He further added that they both liked crack. We know this for sure that the Diablos were trafficking drugs and minimally could have even offered money to either the Dominellos or the police or even both to wind up my dead father hanging in a closet. So, someone is not telling the truth, and in my opinion, someone is lying. After a few more calls, even Detective Pakonis became nasty and said he did not remember anything and would not like to give any statement. He had the nerve to say he did not want to bring dishonor to his name by giving a statement for my book when I was only trying to get closure.

I do not know if my faith is strong enough to believe that the only other place where I can see my father, if it's not on earth, is heaven. I am looking to get some closure from writing my story in this book, but it just seems that so much time has passed, and everything seems to slip like sand from one's hand. I have had another motorcycle gang *Hells Angels,* come to me and say that the Diablos killed my father. Still, I don't know, and even if I do, how can I prove that? Has it drained me to think that did the police cover it up? Why? Why did they not do a thorough investigation? Why not even a single cop or the detective from the Meriden, Southington, or Federal police cared to question a hanging body of their informant? If I being a teenager, can gather up the courage to walk into the clubhouse of the Diablos, then why can't the police.

My entire life starting from the day of my father's death to the time I am writing this book, I have sought truth and justice for my father. There are still horrific photos of my father's corpse lying in the medical examiner record that I have not received, and neither would they hand them over to me. So, my entire youth was spent searching for even the least piece of information that could lead me to that one person who could say that I am the one who is responsible for ruining your life and the life of your father. Unfortunately, no one could ever bring back the time when I was supposed to be living instead of surviving.

I cannot sleep knowing that someone might be taking secrets of my father's murder to their grave. The police can easily forget, but I cannot because I am the one who lost his father-- his strength. I have seen so many hardships, faced near-death experiences, rolled with the scariest gang members seeking answers for my father's murder. I spent numerous sleepless nights, and even now, it is 3:48 a.m., and I am writing this book, past sex addictions and drug addictions, both that I tried to cope with my father's murder.

Real justice will be served when the potentially corrupt police are exposed to assist the gangs in the drug trade. They killed my father in some manner or are perhaps covering up the death or making it look like a suicide. I wish I could walk up and knock on the door of the Diablos to ask if they killed my father or go to the police to ask if this killing will ever stop; if they would ever stop using people then disposing of them for the knowledge they have. My father was murdered for knowing too much and for being an informant. The reason for his death is the definite combination of these two. I no longer want to blame anyone; rather, I would let righteousness reign and consciousness prevail. I no longer get joy from almost anything.

The last thing is the girl who found the hotel door open; who was she? Was she the same girl who got convicted of murdering another man in Meriden, CT, years later and tried to frame it as a suicide and is currently in prison?

www.ingramcontent.com/pod-product-compliance
Lightning Source LLC
Chambersburg PA
CBHW072144020426
42334CB00018B/1873